WIN

Daily Victory in Christ

STEPHANIE TRAYERS

WIN

Daily Victory in Christ

STEPHANIE TRAYERS

Copyright © 2021 by Stephanie Trayers. All rights reserved.

Cover design by Megan Trayers.

Publishing services provided by Barnabas Books LLC.
www.barnabasbooksonline.com

ISBN: 9798708941206

Scripture quotations marked AMP are taken from the Amplified® Bible Classic. Copyright © 1954, 1958, 1962, 1964, 1965, 1987 by The Lockman Foundation. Used by permission. www.Lockman.org | Scripture quotations marked AMPC are from the Amplified® Bible (AMPC). Copyright © 1954, 1958, 1962, 1964, 1965, 1987 by The Lockman Foundation. Used by permission. www.Lockman.org. | Scripture quotations marked CEB are from the COMMON ENGLISH BIBLE. Copyright © 2011 COMMON ENGLISH BIBLE. Used by permission. All rights reserved. www.CommonEnglishBible.com. | Scripture quotations marked CEV are from the *Holy Bible*, Contemporary English Version. Copyright © 1991, 1992, 1995 by American Bible Society. Used by permission. | Scripture quotations marked CJB are taken from the Complete Jewish Bible by David H. Stern. Copyright © 1998. All rights reserved. Used by permission of Messianic Jewish Publishers, 6120 Day Long Lane, Clarksville, MD 21029. www.messianicjewish.net. | Scripture quotations marked CSB are from the Christian Standard Bible®. Copyright © 2017 by Holman Bible Publishers. Used by permission. Christian Standard Bible® and CSB® are federally registered trademarks of Holman Bible Publishers. | Scripture quotations marked ERV are from the *Holy Bible*, Easy-to-Read Version, International Edition. Copyright © 2013, 2016 by Bible League International. Used by permission. | Scripture quotations marked ESV are from The Holy Bible, English Standard Version® (ESV®), copyright © 2001 by Crossway, a publishing ministry of Good News Publishers. Used by permission. All rights reserved. | Scripture quotations marked EXB are taken from The Expanded Bible. Copyright ©2011 by Thomas Nelson, Inc. Used by permission. All rights reserved. | Scripture quotations marked GNT are taken from the Good News Translation — Second Edition © 1992 by American Bible Society. Used by permission. | Scripture quotations marked GW are from GOD'S WORD, which is a copyrighted work of God's Word to the Nations. Copyright © 1995 by God's Word to the Nations. Used by permission. All rights reserved. Scripture quotations marked ISV are taken from the Holy Bible: International Standard Version® Release 2.0. Copyright © 1996–2013 by the ISV Foundation. Used by permission of Davidson Press, LLC. ALL RIGHTS RESERVED INTERNATIONALLY. | Scripture quotations marked MEV are taken from the Modern English Version. Copyright © 2014 by Military Bible Association.

Used by permission. All rights reserved. | Scripture quotations marked NASB are taken from the NEW AMERICAN STANDARD BIBLE. ® Copyright © 1960, 1962, 1963, 1968, 1971, 1972, 1973, 1975, 1977, 1995 by The Lockman Foundation. Used by permission. | Scripture quotations marked NCV are taken from the New Century Version®. Copyright © 2005 by Thomas Nelson, Inc. Used by permission. All rights reserved. | Scripture quotations marked NET are from the NET Bible® (New English Translation). http://netbible.com, copyright ©1996, 2019, used with permission from Biblical Studies Press, L.L.C. All rights reserved. | Scripture quotations marked NIV are from the *Holy Bible*, New International Version®, NIV®. Copyright © 1973, 1978, 1984, 2011 by Biblica, Inc.™ Used by permission of Zondervan. All rights reserved worldwide. www.zondervan.com. The "NIV" and "New International Version" are trademarks registered in the United States Patent and Trademark Office by Biblica, Inc.™ | Scripture quotations marked NKJV are from the New King James Version®. Copyright © 1982 by Thomas Nelson. Used by permission. All rights reserved. | Scripture quotations marked NLT are from the *Holy Bible*, New Living Translation. Copyright © 1996, 2004, 2015 by Tyndale House Foundation. Used by permission of Tyndale House Publishers, Inc., Carol Stream, Illinois 60188. All rights reserved. | Scripture quotations marked NMB are taken from The New Matthew Bible, a special project of Baruch House Publishing. Copyright © 2016. (www.newmatthewbible.org) | Scripture quotations marked Phillips are taken from the PHILLIPS MODERN ENGLISH BIBLE, by J. B. Phillips, "The New Testament in Modern English," Copyright © 1962 edition, published by HarperCollins. | Scripture quotations marked TLB are taken from The Living Bible. Copyright © 1971. Used by permission of Tyndale House Publishers, a Division of Tyndale House Ministries, Carol Stream, Illinois 60188. All rights reserved. | Scripture quotations marked TPT are from The Passion Translation®. Copyright © 2017, 2018 by Passion & Fire Ministries, Inc. Used by permission. All rights reserved. ThePassionTranslation.com. | Scripture quotations marked Voice are taken from The Voice™. Copyright © 2008 by Ecclesia Bible Society. Used by permission. All rights reserved. | Scripture quotations marked WE are taken from THE JESUS BOOK — The Bible in Worldwide English. Copyright © 1969, 1971, 1996, 1998 by SOON Educational Publications, Derby DE65 6BN, UK. Used by permission. | Scripture quotations marked WEB are from the World English Bible, public domain. | Scripture quotations marked WNT 2012 ed. are taken from the The New Testament in Modern Speech by Richard Francis Weymouth, Copyright © 2012. Harrison House Publishers. | Scripture quotations marked Wuest are taken from The New Testament: An Expanded Translation by Kenneth S. Wuest. Copyright © 1961. Wm. B. Eerdmans Publishing Co. All rights reserved.

CONTENTS

INTRODUCTION ix

PART I
Understanding Our Victory in Christ Before Spiritual Attacks

CHAPTER 1: Assemble the Truths 1
CHAPTER 2: Understand Satan's Defeat 7
CHAPTER 3: Use Your Authority 11
CHAPTER 4: Set Your Mind 15
CHAPTER 5: Believe Resurrection Realities 19

PART II
Using Our Victory in Christ During Spiritual Attacks

CHAPTER 6: Fight 25
CHAPTER 7: Resist 29
CHAPTER 8: Know 33
CHAPTER 9: Block 37
CHAPTER 10: Tighten 41
CHAPTER 11: Hold 45
CHAPTER 12: Endure 49

CHAPTER 13: Tread   53
CHAPTER 14: Stand   57

PART III
Enjoying Our Victory in Christ in Everyday Life

CHAPTER 15: Walk in the Victory   63
CHAPTER 16: Thrill in the Power   67
CHAPTER 17: Look Up and Inside   71
CHAPTER 18: Go to God's Words   75
CHAPTER 19: Remember It's the Same   79
CHAPTER 20: View the Glory   83
CHAPTER 21: Make Room for Victory   87

CONCLUSION   91
ABOUT THE AUTHOR   95

INTRODUCTION

Christ followers are on a spiritual and natural journey through life. Jesus came for all of it, not just the spiritual side, but the natural as well. He cares about those feelings, struggles, and challenges we face in our daily lives. But His answers come from a place that is not natural or earthly. His answers are spiritual (heavenly) truths that can greatly affect and transform our natural situations.

The book of Revelation promises rewards to those who overcome or *win*. Of course, there are many days when we feel like we're not winning, days we feel like we're just making it and barely getting through. But our mindset, not our feelings, on these days determines our win.

Wins come through fights. It would be nice to just go through life enjoying God and the peace He gives us. But the truth is there is a spiritual enemy who hates us. The Bible calls him the god of this world and the father of lies (see 2 Corinthians 4:4 and John 8:44). His influence is in full operation, much of the time even affecting our lives as Christians who have been delivered from his power by Christ. If we do not know the truth of his defeat and do something about it, he will continue to rule in many situations in our lives. But what *can* we do about our spiritual enemy?

1 John 5:4–5 (NLT) says, *"For every child of God defeats this evil world, and we achieve this victory through our faith. And who can win this battle against the world? Only those who believe that Jesus is the Son of God."*

I want to point out a few things here. First, *every* child of God defeats the world. This is not a natural ability any of us have, but it comes to us through Jesus' victory over sin and Satan on the cross. Second, we can achieve this victory only through our faith. That's the part *we* have to do. And third, notice that only those people who believe that Jesus is the Son of God are winning this spiritual battle. There is no victory over this evil world anywhere else or through anyone else. If we believers aren't winning this battle, then no one is.

I also like the GOD'S WORD Translation of verse 4: *"… everyone who has been born from God has won the victory over the world. Our faith is what wins the victory over the world"* (emphasis added).

Let me give you an example of the first time this biblical principle worked for me. I was a teenager sitting alone in my car at a stoplight when the familiar feeling of depression began to come over me. But this time something different happened. Months earlier, I had begun to meditate on verses that spoke of the good things God said about me. Over time, those scriptures dropped into my heart and suddenly this time when I felt the depression, words came up out of my heart, into my mind, and out of my mouth as I quoted Psalms 23:6

(KJV), "*Surely goodness and mercy shall follow me all the days of my life: and I will dwell in the house of the Lord for ever.*" Immediately the feeling of depression left me, and I sat there thinking, "Wow, that *really* worked!"

That was many years ago, but I discovered a truth that day that has been confirmed often since then: For us to truly enjoy the life Christ came to give, we must use our faith, which is simply believing God's Word over our circumstances, feelings, or mental reasoning. You see, Jesus won our victory, so we have *already* won. But our faith is what *causes* His victory to become a reality in our daily lives!

The world has no victory for us. As a matter of fact, the world we live in is a dark world and getting darker every day. Jesus told us in Luke 17 that the day would come when we would wish we could see even one day of Jesus here on the earth. But, He said we would not see it. He did, however, give us a truth in this passage about what to do when these dark days would arrive. He said, "*The kingdom of God does not come with observation. Nor will they say, 'Here it is!' or 'There it is!' For remember, the kingdom of God is within you*" (Luke 17:20–21 MEV, emphasis added).

The kingdom of God is within us, so our victory in Christ is within us. We can have personal victory in this life — even while living in a world full of darkness — if we remember not to look outside of ourselves for victory, but to look within our hearts, where Christ lives.

The chapters in *Win* are strategies for spiritual victory in life. You'll notice a particular theme throughout the book: Christians have victory over the forces of darkness through Jesus' victory over these forces in His death, burial, and resurrection. Part I helps you understand your victory in Christ before spiritual attacks. Part II explains how to use that victory during spiritual attacks. Each chapter in this section focuses on a one-word action you can take to battle your spiritual enemy during challenging times. Part III shows you how to enjoy your victory in Christ every day.

His victory is greater than anything we face in this life, and at any time our thoughts can go to the facts of this victory, assuring ourselves of the greatest win this world has ever known!

PART I

Understanding Our Victory in Christ Before Spiritual Attacks

CHAPTER 1

ASSEMBLE THE TRUTHS

There are many great truths in the Word for us. As we go through life, it would do us well to study various biblical subjects that can help us grow in our faith. When it comes to the subject of victory, we need to understand certain truths about what happened to Jesus when He died for us and what happened to us when we received Him as our Savior.

Colossians 2 sums up our victory in Christ:

> **You were spiritually dead because of your sins and because you were not free from the power of your sinful self. But God gave you new life together with Christ. He forgave all our sins. Because we broke God's laws, we owed a debt — a debt that listed all the rules we failed to follow. But God forgave us of that debt. He took**

> **it away and nailed it to the cross. He defeated the rulers and powers of the spiritual world. With the cross he won the victory over them and led them away, as defeated and powerless prisoners for the whole world to see.**
> **(Colossians 2:13–15 ERV)**

Let's take a brief look at what happened when Jesus died, what happened when He rose, and what happened when He was seated.

- When Christ died, He became sin for us. When we received Him as our Savior, our sins were forgiven and our sinful self died. Therefore, Jesus broke the devil's power over us.[1]

- After He paid the price for our sin, Jesus rose, by resurrection power from God, with our justification. When we received Jesus, we rose with Him to a new life that is free from the power of darkness.[2]

- When Jesus went back to heaven, God seated Him at His right hand, far above all evil forces. When we received Jesus, we were seated with Him in this heavenly position, far above all evil forces that could touch our lives while living on earth.[3]

As we can see, we are identified *with Jesus* in all these spiritual acts. When He died, we died. When He rose, we rose. When He was seated, we were seated. This is our true identity in Christ, and these are foundational truths for the subject of victory.

In baking, there are some basic ingredients that just about all recipes call for — flour, sugar, and eggs. Other ingredients are added as well, but just about all recipes require the same basic ingredients. When it's time to make that cake or pie or cookie, bakers will assemble the same basic ingredients every time.

In the same way, the basic ingredients for us to enjoy victory in Christ will always be the same. We must assemble these truths in our hearts: *Jesus died for us, has risen, and is seated. When we received Christ, we died to sin, were risen, and were seated.* There are many other truths in God's Word we can add to these, but these facts are our basic ingredients when it comes to enjoying victory in our lives. We can always go back to these truths when we face challenges that tell us we are defeated.

It's important to think about not only what Jesus did for us but also what happened to us at the same time.

It's important to think about not only what Jesus did *for* us but also what happened *to* us at the same time. The truths that we were buried, risen, and seated are real. They are not things that are going to happen one day when we go to heaven. They are the facts of what already happened to us when we received Christ as our Savior.

Assembling these truths before we face a battle is like stocking our spiritual shelves with ingredients for victory. Meditating on them during the battle can lift us out of our defeated attitude and bring us into a peaceful assurance that God definitely is for us and the victory is ours!

Scripture References

1. *For He made Him who knew no sin to be sin for us, that we might become the righteousness of God in Him.* (2 Corinthians 5:21 NKJV)

   For you died, and your life is hidden with Christ in God. (Colossians 3:3 NKJV)

   Since the children have flesh and blood, he too shared in their humanity so that by his death he might break the power of him who holds the power of death — that is, the devil ... (Hebrews 2:14 NIV)

2. *... That power is the same as the mighty strength he exerted when he raised Christ from the dead and seated him at his right hand in the heavenly realms, far above all rule and authority, power and dominion, and every name that is invoked, not only in the present age but also in the one to come.* (Ephesians 1:19–21 NIV)

   He who was delivered over because of our transgressions, and was raised because of our justification. (Romans 4:25 NASB)

   Buried with Him in baptism, in which also you were raised with Him through the faith of the power of God, who has raised Him from the dead. (Colossians 2:12 MEV)

   Therefore we were buried with Him by baptism into death, that just as Christ was raised up from the dead by the glory of the Father, even so we also should walk in newness of life. (Romans 6:4 MEV)

He has delivered us from the power of darkness and has transferred us into the kingdom of His dear Son. (Colossians 1:13 MEV)

3. *... he raised Christ from the dead and seated him at his right hand in the heavenly realms, far above all rule and authority, power and dominion, and every name that is invoked, not only in the present age but also in the one to come. And God placed all things under his feet and appointed him to be head over everything for the church.*
(Ephesians 1: 20–22 NIV)

But God, being rich in mercy, because of the great love with which he loved us, even when we were dead in our trespasses, made us alive together with Christ — by grace you have been saved — and raised us up with him and seated us with him in the heavenly places in Christ Jesus. (Ephesians 2:4–6 ESV)

We know that everyone who has been born of God does not keep on sinning, but he who was born of God protects him, and the evil one does not touch him. (1 John 5:18 ESV)

CHAPTER 2

UNDERSTAND SATAN'S DEFEAT

I want to share with you a passage of scripture that has helped me understand a truth I had heard many times through the years. Did you ever have a teacher who helped you understand a subject that otherwise would be difficult? Maybe you didn't get it the first time she explained it, so she used a different example to help you grasp it? Well, that's what one translation of a passage in Colossians has done for me.

We know the facts: Jesus died on the cross for us, and our sins are forgiven. But just like a good teacher, God wants us to *understand* the "why" and "how" of Satan's defeat so that we can really grasp the truth about our victory.

We discussed Colossians 2:13–15 in Chapter 1. The New Living Translation says, *"You were dead because of your sins and because your sinful nature was not yet cut away. Then God made you alive with Christ, for he forgave all our sins. He canceled the record of the charges against us and took it away by nailing it to the cross. In this way, he disarmed the spiritual rulers and authorities. He shamed them publicly by his victory over them on the cross."*

I've read this passage many times through the years and in different translations. But this translation brought something to light for me that I had never seen before. These three words jumped off the page: *in this way.*

"In this way" brings together two important truths. The first truth is that God forgave our sins and nailed them to the cross. The second truth is that He disarmed our spiritual enemies. "In this way" tells us *how* God disarmed these evil forces. He disarmed them by nailing our sins to the cross with Jesus.

Adam started out sinless and had dominion over the earth (see Genesis 1:26–28). But Romans 5:12 (CEB) tells us that death entered the world when Adam sinned: *"Just as through one human being sin came into the world, and death came through sin, so death has come to everyone, since everyone has sinned."*

> God disarmed the enemy and took from him the weapons he uses to fight against us.

Sin brought death and evil into the world, and they have been in the world ever since. So *sin* is what the enemy has against us. It is what he's been armed with since Adam first sinned. But when God forgave our sins — nailing them to the cross — God disarmed the enemy and took from him the weapons he uses to fight against us.

Jesus said in Luke 11:21–22 (AMP), "*When the strong man, fully armed, guards his own house, his belongings are undisturbed and secure. But when someone stronger than he attacks and overpowers him, he robs him of all his armor on which he had relied and divides his [goods as] spoil.*"

Satan's "goods" of demonic activity were undisturbed, but Someone stronger than Satan (Jesus) overpowered him and took from him the armor he was relying on. What was the armor he was relying on? Our sins! Jesus overcame him by taking our sins upon Himself and being crucified on the cross.

God wants us to understand this truth of our salvation: When we received Jesus Christ as our Savior, our sins were forgiven, so evil forces now have nothing to fight against us with. They are disarmed. When they threaten to harm us, we need to go back and remind ourselves and them that they have been defeated and disarmed. All of our sins, our shortcomings, our mistakes, and our failures were *nailed to the cross with Jesus!* In this way, God disarmed our spiritual enemies. In this way, we enjoy victory through Jesus!

CHAPTER 3

USE YOUR AUTHORITY

Let's think about Jesus' awesome ministry while He was on earth. If He was present, evil spirits knew it. They would cry out and beg Him not to torment them. He would cast them out with just a word. He healed every kind of sickness and disease. He performed miracles — from turning water into wine, to feeding thousands, to walking on water. And most amazingly, He even raised people from the dead. (See Mark 5:6–7; Matthew 8:16; Matthew 4:23; John 2:1–11; Matthew 14:13–21, 14:22–33; and John 11:1–44.)

Jesus did all of that, yet there was something He did not have — something He would not be given until His time on earth was finished. That something was *all authority*. He said in Matthew 28:18 (MEV), *"All authority has been given to Me in heaven and on earth."* Jesus made this statement after He rose from the dead but before He went to heaven to sit at the right hand of God.

It's an astounding thought — *all authority given to Him in heaven and on earth.*

Have you ever wondered why Jesus needed that authority? It would make sense to hear Him make such a statement *before* He began His ministry. But He said it, not before He began His ministry on earth, but after it was finished.

Jesus said, "*All authority has been given to Me in heaven and on earth.*" Then He left and went to heaven.

Did Jesus need that authority? Did He need more authority than what He had while He was ministering on earth? Look at all the powerful things He did in His life without being given all authority in heaven and earth. What good would all authority do now that He was leaving? Why was more given to Him when He would not be on earth any longer?

The fact is, Jesus did not need any more authority than what He had. He was with God at the beginning of time, and He even saw Satan being cast out of heaven (see Luke 10:18). Jesus had all the authority He needed when He performed all those miracles and healings. When He was present, the devil experienced defeat in one way or another.

Jesus could cast out demons and do all those miracles without having all authority. So what is this "all authority" then? He had authority over evil spirits, sickness, disease, and even death, so what authority did He *not* have? What was this "all authority" that He died to obtain?

"All authority" refers to the authority that man would need to win in life. The authority that man would need to use over evil since Jesus would not be physically present. The authority that was never available in all the years before Jesus' death and resurrection. Mankind authority through Jesus Christ.

When Jesus made the statement, *"All authority has been given to Me in heaven and on earth,"* it was more than just a way to say goodbye. He intentionally spoke those words as He was leaving the earth so that His followers would not have to go back to the way things were before He lived and ministered among them.

Another time Jesus said, *"Look, I give you authority to trample on serpents and scorpions, and over all the power of the enemy. And nothing shall by any means hurt you"* (Luke 10:19 MEV). This tells us that the authority Jesus is speaking of is for us to use over any evil that would interfere with peace in our lives, homes, or families. We can use our authority over any situation that tries to steal, kill, or destroy the full, abundant life Jesus came to bring us (see John 10:10).

And yet much of the time we are hesitant to use our God-given authority in our daily lives. But we must realize that He gave it for us to use. This authority is ours to use as we need to in life. Reading the entire passage of Matthew 28:18–20, we see that Jesus entrusted believers with the authority He was given, telling us to go make, baptize, and teach disciples. In whatever we do for Christ, we are supplied with the authority to do it. Jesus said, *"All authority has been given to Me in heaven and on earth. <u>Go</u> therefore ... "* (Matthew 28:18–19, emphasis added). "Go" is an action. Jesus is telling us to go with our authority, *act* on our authority, *move* in our authority, and *use* our authority. If we want to benefit from the authority Jesus provided for us over the works of the enemy, we will have to *do* something with the authority He gave us.

> *The act of using our authority is what ensures that evil cannot harm us.*

Let's look a little closer at Luke 10:19. Notice that Jesus didn't say that He gave us authority over evil and that nothing would hurt us. He said He gave us authority to *trample* over the enemy and that nothing would hurt us. Again, the authority has been given for us to use. The action of *trampling* on the enemy — the act of *using* our authority — is what ensures that evil cannot harm us.

So when Jesus paid the price for our sins, all authority was given *to* Him, not *for* Him because He didn't need anymore. The authority was given to Jesus *for us*. Everything He did, He did for us. That's why He said these words right before He left earth. With Jesus no longer on earth, His followers would now need that authority. Whenever we are faced with evil or the effects of evil, we can use the authority that Jesus won *for us*!

CHAPTER 4

SET YOUR MIND

Our position in Christ is something we may not think about very often. The thought may come to us when we hear a message in church or read certain scriptures, but our position in Christ is not a thought that's usually on most of our minds.

Ephesians 2:4–6 (WEB) says, "But God, being rich in mercy, for his great love with which he loved us, even when we were dead through our trespasses, made us alive together with Christ — by grace you have been saved — and raised us up with him, and made us to sit with him in the heavenly places in Christ Jesus."

God wants the truth about where we are positioned to be on our minds. Colossians 3:1–2 (NIV) says, "Since, then, you have been raised with Christ, set your hearts on things above, where Christ is, seated at the right hand of God. *Set your minds on things above, not on earthly things."*

Putting those two passages together, we see that God raised us up *with* Jesus. At the *same time* He raised Jesus, He raised every born-again believer. Now we are to set our minds on things above. We are to set our minds on Jesus being seated in heaven and on our being seated with Him. That sounds very deep and spiritual (and it is!), but it is actually a thought that should be on our minds.

But what in the world does that thought have to do with our daily lives? Why does it matter when we have so many other things on our minds, important things like work, school, our families, and all that we have to get done today? Spiritual thoughts are fine at church and in our private devotions, but how do they fit into our busy world? How can the Bible tell us not to set our minds on the things of earth, but on heavenly things? How can any person living in this busy world even do that?

The key is in that little word *set*. We are told to set our minds on these things. The Wuest translation says to *"be constantly setting your mind"* on things above. It's obvious that we cannot keep our minds on spiritual truths constantly, but we should constantly *keep setting* our minds there, going back to these thoughts in between the many other thoughts our minds are busy with throughout the day.

These thoughts of our spiritual position are important because they are the *truth*. They are "truth thoughts." Philippians 4:8 (EXB) gives us a list of things to think about, and truth is at the top of the list: *"think about [focus your thoughts on; fill your minds with] things that are true ..."* And although we have many other things to think about, our thoughts should always come back home to the truth. Just like we all love to come home after a busy day at work and just relax, our minds need to constantly come back home to the *truth* and relax in the reality of our position in Christ.

> We are seated with Jesus, far above any evil forces that try to come against our lives.

We are seated with Christ in the spirit realm, and He is seated far above all spiritual rulers and powers of this world. To think about our position right next to Him is to realize that any evil that tries to affect our lives is actually far below us! We are seated with Jesus, far above any evil forces that try to come against our lives.

Thinking about these truths is a challenge because our minds do not naturally think about heavenly things. That's why we must keep focusing our minds on these truth thoughts. If we don't constantly set our minds back on them, these truths will never become real to us like God intended them to.

We can take thoughts likes these from Ephesians 2 and Colossians 3 and keep going back to them in our minds throughout the day. It will allow our minds to enjoy a break from the busyness of life and go home to the truth. As we continue to set our minds on things above, something wonderful will begin to happen. In the same way spending time in our natural home refreshes us so that we can go back out into our busy world, spending time reflecting on our true position in Christ will refresh our minds with peace, joy, and a new perspective as we go back to the thoughts of our day.

CHAPTER 5

BELIEVE RESURRECTION REALITIES

Luke 24:1–11 describes the resurrection of Jesus. Women brought spices to the tomb early on Sunday morning, but the huge stone that covered the entrance had been rolled aside and Jesus' body was gone. Two angels appeared and asked the women this:

> "Why are you looking in a tomb for someone who is alive? He isn't here! He has come back to life again! Don't you remember what he told you back in Galilee — that the Messiah must be betrayed into the power of evil men and be crucified and that he would rise again the third day?" Then they remembered and rushed back to Jerusalem to tell his

eleven disciples — and everyone else — what had happened." (Luke 24: 5–9 TLB)

Jesus had told his disciples that he was going to die and rise again. But when the women came and told them that He had indeed risen, verse 11 says, *"the story sounded like a fairy tale to the men — they didn't believe it."*

The 11 disciples eventually all believed and even saw Jesus for themselves. At first though, the story that Jesus had risen from the dead seemed made up. But before we are quick to judge the disciples for not immediately believing, let's look at another resurrection that some of us don't fully believe yet — our own.

Colossians 2:12 (CEB) says, *"You were buried with him through baptism and raised with him through faith in the power of God, who raised him from the dead."* Did you catch that? We were raised with Jesus.

But all too often, the idea that we have been raised with Christ sounds like a fairy tale to us as we think about all the realities of our natural life. Family, school, work, finances, our health — these are the realities that we deal with every day. Resurrection sounds like something we'll be thinking about when our life is coming to an end and we're about to go to heaven. But actually, we *were* resurrected with Christ. *Were* is in the past tense; this resurrection has already happened. When Jesus was raised from the dead, we were raised *with Him*.

Does this still sound like a fairy tale, considering all the realities of life you're dealing with? Remember that we must focus on the truth, not just our situations. In the previous chapter, we saw the importance of setting our minds on things above. Let's read those verses from Colossians 3:1–2 in the Passion Translation:

> **Christ's resurrection is your resurrection too. This is why we are to yearn for all that is above, for that's where Christ sits enthroned at the place of all power, honor, and authority! Yes, feast on all the treasures of the heavenly realm and fill your thoughts with heavenly realities, and not with the distractions of the natural realm.**

Jesus was resurrected, but the disciples did not know it at first and were focused on the darkness and sadness of the hour. So when they heard that Jesus was risen, they thought it was nonsense and that the women who had been at the tomb were making up stories.

Our resurrection with Christ is our reality.

When our thoughts are on the darkness of the day we're living in or when we are distracted by this natural realm, heavenly realities seem like something made up. They just seem like fairy tales. But this news is too important not to believe. Our resurrection with Christ *is* our reality. Circumstances will come and go, but these heavenly realities remain true.

The Bible instructs us to feast on the treasures of the heavenly realm. Our minds can feast on thoughts of Jesus being seated at the right hand of God, enthroned in power, and positioned above every evil thing that exists. We can fill our minds with thoughts like our own seating next to Him in that heavenly place (see Ephesians 1:20–22, 2:4–6).

If we're hearing these truths for the first time or haven't thought about them in a while, they may seem too good to be true. God did raise us with Christ, but we will never enjoy the reality of this position if we don't do our part.

The Bible's instructions are clear about what our part is. We are to fill our thoughts with these "heavenly realities." By keeping these thoughts in our minds, we'll stay in victory no matter what's going on around us.

The disciples eventually experienced the joy of Jesus' resurrection. Likewise, the more we think about this truth, the more we will experience the joy of being raised with Christ!

PART II

Using Our Victory in Christ During Spiritual Attacks

CHAPTER 6

FIGHT

The Christian life is not just a walk. It's also a war. Second Corinthians 10:3–4 (GW) says, *"Of course we are human, but we don't fight like humans. The weapons we use in our fight are not made by humans. Rather, they are powerful weapons from God."* In other words, we're just human beings, but that doesn't mean that we fight like human beings. The Phillips Modern English Bible says that although *"we lead normal human lives, the battle we are fighting is on the spiritual level."*

Don't think this war is just for ministers or for very spiritual people. Every one of us who has received Christ is in a spiritual war, although we are human and living normal human lives. And we are all going to have to *fight*.

But that's not bad news! First Timothy 6:12 (NIV) tells us to *"Fight the good fight of faith."* It is a good fight because Jesus has already defeated our enemies, but it is a fight of *faith*. When we decide we are going to live by faith (the truths of God's Word), then the fight is on.

Spiritual battles test our faith. Spiritual battles test our faith; our faith is what the enemy fights against. Have you ever noticed that when our spiritual enemy attacks us with condemnation and defeat, the first thing we want to give up on is what we have been doing *spiritually?* We don't start putting aside natural things like going to work and taking care of our home and family. Instead, we're immediately tempted to give up on the spiritual things we have been doing, like praying, spending time in the Word, and maybe even going to church. That's the enemy's tactic; he is fighting our faith.

Ephesians 6:12 (CEV) tells us that we are fighting against these spiritual enemies, not against human beings: *"We are not fighting against humans. We are fighting against forces and authorities and against rulers of darkness and powers in the spiritual world."*

Think about arm wrestling. For a while, the opponents' forearms are upright with their hands wrapped around the others'. Each wrestler uses his strength to push his opponent's arm down. And each one feels the pressure of his opponent's strength. In the same way, we know that we are wrestling spiritually when we feel the oppression and pressure coming against us. We feel the strength of our spiritual enemy. He is pressing hard with his works in our lives or in the lives of people around us.

In the course of the attack, we may feel like we are losing. We will feel the enemy's pressure and his blows, and we may feel as if we have been badly beaten, bruised, and bloodied. But that doesn't mean we're losing! It just means that we are in a fight. At the end of a fight, both fighters look beaten up — but one is the victor. And in this fight of faith, we are the victors!

But this fight will not be based on our own goodness, strength, or ability. We will have to fight solely with New Testament truths. We war by holding firmly to truths like what Jesus did to Satan when He died and rose again, what God says about us now that we are new people in Christ, what our position is in Christ, and what we can do through Christ.

You see, when we fight with the simple truths of victory in Christ we feel the attack, but at the very same time our enemy feels *his* opponent — us! He feels it when we take New Testament truth — the one thing he absolutely cannot stand — and fight with it. He feels the pressure of us using our authority in Christ. He feels the sting of our sword, the Word of God. He feels the strength of our grip as we hold on tight to what God said. He feels us enforcing our victory in Christ.

So the next time you feel the pressure of your spiritual enemy, think about what *he's* feeling as he fights *you!*

CHAPTER 7

RESIST

The Bible describes Satan in several ways, but I want to focus on two. John 10:10 (NIV) says, *"The thief comes only to steal and kill and destroy; I have come that they may have life, and have it to the full."* And 1 Peter 5:8 (NKJV) says, *"... your adversary the devil walks about like a roaring lion, seeking whom he may devour."*

Usually a thief is quiet, but the Bible explains that this thief is also a lion. When he comes to steal, kill, and destroy, he roars, yells, and screams. So our spiritual enemy is a loud, demanding thief. Jesus came that we would have an abundant life that is full of peace, joy, and victory. But Satan comes to steal, kill, or destroy any life-giving thing that God has blessed us with, and he does it through roaring.

Here's what I mean by roaring. The enemy comes at us in a demanding and loud way. He can work through the actions and words of others, past experiences, our own shortcomings and mistakes, physical symptoms and pain, bad news, and all other kinds of circumstances. These attacks come at us like a roaring lion. They demand our attention and make us feel as if we must give in to them because they are so loud in our life. And when we give in and start believing him, this thief actually steals from us. He steals our peace, joy, hope, and victory.

So what can we do about this thief who acts like a lion in our lives?

Looking at 1 Peter 5:8–9 (NKJV), we see God's instructions: *"Be sober, be vigilant; because your adversary the devil walks about like a roaring lion, seeking whom he may devour. Resist him, steadfast in the faith ..."* (emphasis added).

In this passage, we are given steps to *resist* the roar of the enemy in our lives. We are to

- **BE SOBER.** We need to be serious so that we can recognize spiritual attacks. We do not need to think that everything that goes wrong in our lives is the devil. But when our peace, joy, and victory are constantly being attacked, we need to know who is behind it.

- **BE VIGILANT.** We must be spiritually alert and watchful.

- **RESIST HIM.** We must purposefully and intentionally fight the devil off and actively oppose him, for James 4:7 (CEV) says, *"Resist the devil, and he will run from you."*

- **BE STEADFAST.** We must constantly resist the enemy, not just once in a while.

- **Be steadfast IN THE FAITH.** We're not fighting the devil in our own strength, ability, or worthiness. We're resisting him by being firm in our faith in what the Word says about us and in what Jesus did to conquer our enemy.

> We're not fighting the devil in our own strength, ability, or worthiness.

God wants us to understand that the devil comes to steal, kill, and destroy with his loud and demanding roars. That's how this thief works; he combines roaring and stealing. He roars by making the circumstances of our lives seem *really* bad so that we believe him instead of the truth of God's Word. That's how he steals from us.

For instance, we may be enjoying peace in our lives, but then comes a roar that sounds and feels bigger than that peace. That roar is going to seem so big that the temptation to give in will be great. But if we give in, he steals and robs us of our peace, our joy, and our assurance that God is a good God and that He is for us.

We must remember that it's just a roar. Yelling and screaming at us through our circumstances is the enemy's way of demanding our attention and causing us to feel greatly defeated. But that roar is not the TRUTH.

I don't know what that roar looks like in your life. It's different for everyone, but the steps for victory are the same for all of us: *Be sober, be vigilant, resist him, be steadfast,* and do it *in the faith* of what God's Word says. If you follow those steps, your enemy will turn and go away while you continue to enjoy your abundant life in Jesus.

CHAPTER 8

KNOW

Second Corinthians 10:5 (NIV) says, *"We demolish arguments and every pretension that sets itself up against the knowledge of God, and we take captive every thought to make it obedient to Christ."*

The spiritual battle we fight is between the knowledge of God (what His Word says) and any thought that comes against this knowledge. The enemy comes against God's own Word that you and I have chosen to believe. He wants us to doubt that what God said is really true.

But I think God would ask all of us, "Why do you let his lies affect you at all? Why don't you just take those thoughts from the enemy captive as soon as they enter your mind? Why do you let life's interruptions defeat you so quickly? I've given you My Word and My Spirit to guide and empower you. So what have I *not* given you for victory? What have I *not* given you to succeed?"

I think if we were being honest we would have to say, "God, I don't *feel* like I have victory." But 2 Peter 1:3 (KJV) says that His power has given us everything we need for life and godliness "... *through the knowledge of Him*" (emphasis added) — not through *feelings*. But there's no denying that our feelings greatly affect us.

When lies come into our minds, they come with *feelings* to back them up: feelings of fear, feelings of failure, feelings of defeat, feelings of strife, feelings of struggle, feelings of lack. That's why the enemy's lies seem more real than the Word at times. They seem to be the truth, but they are actually wrong thoughts coming against the Word of God we have chosen to believe.

Maybe you, like me, have enjoyed *good* feelings of peace and joy that come from God's blessings. But I have discovered that most of the time in the midst of the battle, the knowledge of God — that is, the Word of God that you and I are believing, doesn't come with any feelings. And that's what makes this fight ... a fight.

I want to share a simple truth that has helped me through some of the most challenging battles I have faced. It is this: In the heat of the battle, we must fight *feelings* with *knowledge*. At times it will seem like the lie is the truth because it will *feel* bigger, more powerful, and more real than the knowledge of the Word.

Fight with what you know.

But when you are armed with the understanding that knowledge does not come with feelings, you will be strengthened to face those situations with a greater determination. It's not going to *feel* any different. It's not going to *feel* like it's true. You are going to *feel* like giving up. But fight with what you *know*.

The Word of God is more powerful than what you feel, and it is the truth. When you realize the Word that you're standing on does not have feelings and you take those wrong thoughts captive, the battle will soon be over. And you will win again!

CHAPTER 9

BLOCK

Ephesians 6 gives us instructions for how to handle the attacks that are going to come from our spiritual enemy. Verse 16 tells us, *"In every situation take up the shield of faith with which you can extinguish all the flaming arrows of the evil one"* (CSB).

These flaming arrows are not natural. They are attacks that come against us in the unseen realm. Our faith is the shield that protects us from these attacks.

The shield of faith is a response of faith.

The shield of faith is a *response* of faith. When we respond to the attack with what the Word of God says about the situation, the enemy's arrow cannot penetrate. We may still feel the pain of the attack, but we walk by faith — not by sight or feelings — and that initial feeling will soon disappear as we continue to focus on what the Word says (see 2 Corinthians 5:7).

Blocking the enemy's attacks with the truth of God's Word reminds me of a volleyball game. Players send the ball back and forth over the net, but there's a play that really gets our attention. It's when one player spikes the ball across the net with such force that it looks like there's no way the ball can be blocked. But someone on the other team is in position to block that spike, so the opposing team does not get a point. Those two opposing players are usually very skilled and make the game exciting for us to watch.

I hate to break it to you, but our spiritual enemy is shooting arrows at us with great skill. We may feel unqualified and wonder why and how we got in the position to have to block his spikes (or arrows) against us. But regardless of what we may think or feel, as followers of Christ we are in this position. Blocking the enemy's attacks is our challenge.

To stay in victory when the attacks come, we must always be in position to block the next arrow from the enemy. That may sound impossible, but the Bible shows us how to do it: *"Prepare your minds for action"* (1 Peter 1:13 NLT). In other words, as the Complete Jewish Bible says, *"Get your minds ready for work."*

You see, the lie will be crafted just for you. It will be tailored to your past, your hurts, your weaknesses, and your mistakes. Maybe it will be an arrow of what people are saying about you. Or maybe it will be an arrow pointed right at your future — an arrow of what he's going to do to you or someone you love, or an arrow that tells you that you're not going to make it. What are those arrows that you seem to deal with constantly from the enemy?

After you have identified the arrows, prepare your mind with what the Word says that counteracts those lies. Get in position to block the thoughts when they come. We can train ourselves, even as we go about our daily routine, to instantly block the thoughts that come into our minds from the enemy with the truth of God's Word.

And that's how the shield of faith works and protects us. The evil planned against us meets the shield of faith, and the shield extinguishes the evil. Responding in faith makes the arrow disappear.

God has given us this glorious means of victory through the triumph of our Lord Jesus. But notice something else here. The very next verse tells us to take *"the sword of the Spirit — which is the Word of God"* (Ephesians 6:17 CSB). Satan has arrows, but we have a sword, and when we use this sword of the Spirit against him, he cannot block *our* attack. Why? Because Jesus defeated him on the cross!

Get your mind in position to block spiritual attacks with your shield of faith!

CHAPTER 10

TIGHTEN

When my daughter was little, she wanted her belt around her waist to be very tight. Although the belt was her correct size, it still wasn't tight enough for her. She wanted it to feel snug around her waist. Eventually, her dad put extra holes in it, so she could tighten it even more!

> When evil happens in our lives, we should tighten the truth of God's Word.

Ephesians 6:14 (AMPC) tells us to, "*Stand therefore [hold your ground], having <u>tightened</u> the belt of truth around your loins*" (emphasis added). When evil happens in our lives, we should tighten the truth of God's Word.

But when circumstances get bad and we start experiencing evil, we tend to *loosen* the truth of victory in our minds. When we loosely think about the truths of our victory, the temptation to focus on our circumstances becomes greater. Like a loose belt, we believe the truth, but it's just not as snug as it should be.

Hebrews 2:1 (GW) says, "... *we must pay closer attention to what we have heard. Then we won't drift away [from the truth]."* Some translations of this verse say that we can actually let truths slip from us.

During trying times in our lives, we may not have God's Word on tight enough. The truth may still be in us, but it may not be as tight as it was before the attack came. Therefore, we need to do as Hebrews says, *pay closer attention* to the truths we believe. If we don't pay closer attention to God's Word in difficult times, truths that should be tight start to become loose truths in our minds. We drift away from them when we should actually *come closer* to them.

There's no better way to tighten the belt of truth in our minds than by paying closer attention to God's Word. When we are tempted to give up, we should go the other way and tighten the belt of truth by spending more — not less — time in His Word.

Tighten the truth of God's Word around you by spending more time focusing on scriptures that speak to your particular situation. If you have been going through a rough season and feel like giving up, then focus on a truth like this: "... *we are* more than conquerors *through Him who loved us."* (Romans 8:37 MEV, emphasis added).

That's a great truth. Now tighten it a little more by looking at the verse in a different translation. The classic edition of the Amplified Bible says it this way: "... *we are more than conquerors and* gain a surpassing victory *through Him Who loved us"* (emphasis added).

Now let's tighten it even more. The Complete Jewish Bible says this: "... *we are <u>superconquerors</u>, through the one who has loved us*" (emphasis added).

Do you see how we can make the truths tighter and tighter in our minds? When a truth becomes loose in our minds because of the evil around us, we *tighten* that truth. God's Words may start out pretty loose in our minds, but they become tighter and tighter as we take more time to pay closer attention to them.

Just like adding extra holes to a belt, we will experience the tightness of His truth around us so we can win another victory in Him!

CHAPTER 11

HOLD

Let's never lose sight of the awesome victory God has already won for us: *"God stripped the spiritual rulers and powers of their authority. With the cross, he won the victory and showed the world that they were powerless"* (Colossians 2:15 NCV).

And let's also remember that this victory is about Christ:

> **So do not let anyone make rules for you about eating and drinking or about a religious feast, a New Moon Festival, or a Sabbath day. These things were like a shadow of what was to come. But what is true and real has come and is found in Christ. Do not let anyone disqualify you by making you humiliate yourself and worship angels. Such people enter into visions, which fill them with foolish pride because of their human way of thinking. They do not hold tightly to Christ, the head. It is from him that all the parts of the**

body are cared for and held together. So it grows in the way God wants it to grow. (Colossians 2:16–19 NCV)

Isn't that amazing? The examples we read about in the Old Testament were shadows, but Jesus is the reality, or body, of those shadows. And He is higher than any spiritual experience a person can have outside of Him. This passage also emphasizes the importance of holding tightly to Christ.

Holding is trusting.

Holding is trusting. We hold to Christ when we put our trust in Him, when we don't let go of Him. Our trust is in Jesus and the salvation He provides for us. We can think of this in a general way, but when circumstances get bad, it is time to *intentionally* hold tightly to Christ.

When troubles come in our lives, they can come at us fast and out of nowhere. And when they come, we usually don't have time to do a Bible study on how to handle the crisis. There are also times when things come at us unexpectedly, and we don't know where to turn. It may be bad news, a hurtful word, or an upsetting experience. We can be doing just fine, but then something comes along that really interferes with our peace of mind.

But there is something we can do when these challenges come against us, and we can do it fast. The moment we are faced with a challenging circumstance, we can hold on to Jesus. When we feel ourselves going down, we can call out to Him, the Head of the Church.

Jesus is the One who has the power to help us, and He cannot be held down by any evil. Acts 2:24 (EXB) says that even *"death could not hold him."* So the moment we hold to Him, we are staying up and not going down in defeat. Holding tightly to Jesus is like grabbing a heavenly balloon that lifts us up and out of the defeat trying to bring us down.

Troubles may come at us fast, but we have a fast way to deal with them. When we turn to Jesus immediately, we are holding on to our victory. We may feel like we've been defeated, but the truth is Jesus cannot be defeated, and He's the One we're holding on to! This shortcut to victory bypasses condemnation and any of our own efforts to stay in our victorious position.

"Since we have a great High Priest who presides over the house of God ... Let us hold strong to the confession of our hope, never wavering, since the One who promised it to us is faithful" (Hebrews 10:21, 23 Voice).

Our spiritual enemy is trying to get us to let go. But when he tries, we respond by clinging to Jesus. This is not the time to loosen our grip. This is the time to hold tightly to our confession of what God's Word says about us and the circumstance, to hold on to our hope, and to hold on to what we have been praying for. God is faithful! So hold tight, hold strong, and win!

CHAPTER 12

ENDURE

In the book of Hebrews, the writer is speaking to a group of believers who were going through tough times. But he tells them to remember that when they first received Christ, they endured great persecution. He reminds them that although they are going through tough times now, they have been through worse. And during those darker days, the message of Christ was so fresh and alive in them that they endured joyfully.

But what happens with all of us is that time goes on and those experiences of victory fade away. Because the victories are no longer at the forefront of our minds, we are tempted to give up when new storms or troubles come. So the writer tells them in Hebrews 10:35–38 (ESV) *"Therefore do not throw away your confidence, which has a great reward. <u>For you have need of endurance</u>, so that when you have done the will of God you may receive what is promised. For ... 'my righteous one shall live by faith ... '"* (emphasis added).

Have you ever seen one of those police officer shows on TV where one of the officers dies or gets promoted and leaves his or her partner alone? So then it's time for the remaining officer to get a new partner and he goes into the police chief's office and the police chief assigns him or her a new partner. This new partner is usually the complete opposite of the old partner, which sets the stage for how these two new partners will work together.

I once experienced something similar. While praying about some disappointments I was experiencing, the Lord showed me what I needed. It was as if Jesus Himself was sitting at a conference table with me, listening to my complaints. Then he said, "You need Endurance." "Endurance, meet Stephanie. Stephanie, meet your new partner, Endurance."

So what does it mean to endure? *The American Heritage Dictionary*[1] says that it means to

- Carry on through, despite hardships.
- Bear with tolerance.
- Continue in existence.
- Remain.
- Last.
- Put up with.
- Suffer patiently without yielding.
- Persevere.
- Hold out.

One thing I want to point out here is that to truly endure, we must first be sure that we are doing our part to resist the enemy. We must make sure that we are praying and standing on God's Word when life seems to be against us. If we aren't doing those things, then we cannot say that we are enduring — we're just being a doormat for the enemy to walk on. If we bring our problems to God in prayer and stand on the truths of His

Word for our circumstances, we'll begin to see things turn for us and enjoy many victories in our lives.

But there are times in our lives that require endurance. Times when it seems like things are not changing. We have prayed and believed God, but the circumstances stay the same or even get worse. This is when we are tempted to give up, to think that our faith is not working for us. But there's something we need at this very moment, something we've maybe never thought much about before but is a real power to come alongside us in our most trying times: Endurance.

What does it look like to have endurance in tough times? It looks like not having any other assurance that everything is going to be okay except for the Word of God, yet we keep on going. We go about our day like normal, but on the inside we feel as if we're not going to make it through this time. But we keep going.

Going back to our dictionary definitions, having endurance is "to suffer patiently without yielding" to the temptation to quit. We "carry on through, despite hardships." We bear the situation with tolerance. We "hold out." Sometimes we feel as if we're just remaining in existence. Endurance is our partner during such times. When we say, "This is hard," endurance is that virtue that says, "Yes, it's hard; keep going." When we say, "This hurts," it says, "Yes, it hurts; keep going." We say, "Nothing is changing." Endurance says, "Hold on." We say, "This isn't fair." Endurance says, "No, it's not fair; keep going."

Endurance reminds us that God's Word — the truth that we're standing on — is not affected by things not going well. Hebrews 10:32 in the Good News Translation says it this way, "... *you suffered many things yet were not defeated by the struggle.*" You may feel like you're being defeated by the suffering and hardship you're going through, but the struggle is not defeating you, so just endure!

> *Endurance reminds us that God's Word — the truth that we're standing on — is not affected by things not going well.*

Endurance keeps us going through our tough times. When that tough time eventually comes to an end, just picture yourself giving your partner Endurance a high five because you will still be standing when the storm is over and you will be so glad you did not give up!

James 1:2-4 (NLT) gives us even more insight about the result of endurance: "*Dear brothers and sisters, when troubles of any kind come your way, consider it an opportunity for great joy. For you know that when your faith is tested, your endurance has a chance to grow. So let it grow, for when your endurance is fully developed, you will be perfect and complete, needing nothing.*" This is a great promise to stand on. While we are enduring, we are also maturing into who God has called us to be.

Are you going through a tough time? Are you doing what you know to do but nothing is changing? If so, I would like to introduce you to your new partner, Endurance!

1. *The American Heritage Dictionary of the English Language.* Boston: Houghton Mifflin Harcourt, 1973.

CHAPTER 13

TREAD

Every day that we live on this earth we are on a walk. We walk through the seasons of life, with its many ups and downs. Some days are memorable, such as special occasions and holidays. Some days we just go about our normal routine. Some days we feel as if we are not going to make it. Other times, we feel confident that we can handle anything that comes our way. We enjoy some days more than others, but no matter how we feel, as long as we are breathing, we are still walking.

As we walk through this life and through the good and bad that comes our way, Jesus said to focus on a certain type of walking. He said in Luke 10:19 (ESV) that He gives us authority to tread (some translations say *trample*) over all the power of the enemy: *"Behold, I have given you authority to tread on serpents and scorpions, and over all the power of the enemy, and nothing shall hurt you."*

We know that this life is a walk of faith, but what does it mean to *tread*? Treading is a certain *type* of walking.

To tread is to step and walk in a way that presses down heavily so as to crush whatever is underneath it.

We certainly do not have the physical power to trample over our spiritual enemy, and we usually don't feel spiritually strong enough to accomplish something so great. But we need to understand that this treading and trampling is not based on anything we have accomplished or on something we have earned by our spiritual efforts. As a matter of fact, it's much simpler than that.

Have you ever seen a truck tread through rough terrain or seen a herd of animals trampling through fields? They are moving through regardless of what's underneath them. Sadly, we've even heard of people who have been trampled on by other people who were trying to get to the stage at a concert or be the first through the door at an event. That trampling was not about trying to hurt someone else; they were just focused on where they wanted to go, regardless of the people around them. Trucks and herds of animals are not trying to do anything to the ground underneath them; they are just moving through in a heavy, crushing manner as they head to their destination. The treading over something is just the result of a greater thing — the determination of that truck, animal, or person to go somewhere and to get from where they are to where they want to be.

There are times our lives seem to be at their worst, and the ground underneath us feels rough and difficult. We feel like everything is against us and our walk becomes extremely hard. Trampling over our spiritual enemies is a result of our mindset while we walk through these times on our spiritual journey. By focusing with determination on the truths of God's Word, the walk actually becomes a *tread*. We don't do this heavy treading in our own strength. We just use the powerful Word of God in that rough part of our walk.

So what difference does it make whether we tread and trample or whether we just get through the situation? Here's the difference: *treading crushes the thing underneath it.*

> *The enemy, and all his power, is underneath us.*

The enemy, and all his power, is underneath us. The tough times in life that are difficult to walk through are opportunities for us to tread and trample over them! Those enemies of Christ must be walked on and walked over with heavy, firm-footed steps of our assurance in Jesus. We can make it through challenging parts of our walk by being assured of what the Word says. This is how we tread over the spiritual enemies in our lives. Notice we're not *trying* to tread or trample over anything; we just have a focused determination on something else, which causes trampling to occur. Our focused attention on the Word during our rough seasons will cause us to trample over all of our spiritual enemies. What a defeat for them to be trampled on because our focus is on something else — the truth of God's Word! That's the defeat Jesus planned for our enemies when He said we would tread over them.

You're going to go through this tough situation either way. So why not use the situation as an opportunity to crush the enemy under your feet? You will tread for a while, the situation will end, and then you will go back to walking through life on smoother ground.

So you can either *get through* (and barely make it), or you can *tread through* (and win some more victories). The difference is in your mindset while *going through* the rough days in life.

CHAPTER 14

STAND

Ephesians 6:10–14 (WEB) says, "*Finally, be strong in the Lord, and in the strength of his might. Put on the whole armor of God, that you may be able to stand against the wiles of the devil. ... that you may be able to withstand in the evil day, and, having done all, to stand. Stand therefore ... .*"

As you can see, the emphasis in these verses is on standing. As a matter of fact, we are told to stand four times in verses 11–14.

But I want to emphasize the words *having done all*. "Having done all, to stand." Those words imply that there are things we can *do* when we face attacks in life. We can pray and seek God's wisdom. We can respond in faith with the Word of God. We can resist the enemy. We can use our God-given authority. We can *do* what the Word of God tells us to do.

I can tell you there are times in my life when I do not do all to stand. Maybe I try a little, but I don't do all I know to do in the situation. After the attack is over, if I question God about what went wrong, 99% of the time He shows me an area where I didn't do what I needed to do to stand. But when I diligently seek God's wisdom and stand in faith against the attack, I am able to just keep standing until the whole thing is over. You see, those Ephesians 6 verses call attacks "the evil day." It's just a day, a season, a moment, and it will soon be over.

When we've done all we know to do and things don't change for the better or they get worse, we have a decision to make. We must choose between two mindsets. The first mindset says, "I've done all I can do, but it's not better. I just have to give up." The second mindset says, "I've done all I can do, but it's not better. I just have to stand."

Standing holds out. Standing holds on.

Once we've done all to stand, we stand. We don't move. We don't give up when things don't seem to be getting any better. We just stand. Standing is not moving away from victory. Standing holds out. Standing holds on.

I love that those verses don't say to just lie there and take it. No, they tell us to stand. You may be facing something that has knocked you off your feet, but you can get up and stand. Even if you don't feel like you have any strength to stand, you can stand. How do I know? Because verse 10 of Ephesians 6 tells us to be strong in the Lord and in His strength.

Remember, you're not standing in your strength; you're standing in *Jesus'* strength. You're standing in what He said. You're standing in what He did. You see, these are attacks from our spiritual enemy, so now is the time to remind ourselves about what Jesus did about this enemy. First John 3:8 says, *"The reason that the Son of God was revealed was to destroy what the Devil has been doing"* (ISV). We need to stand on truths like these during the attack.

When we try to stand against evil in our own strength, we feel overwhelmed and unable to stand. But we don't need to try to do anything; we just need to stand in His strength. And it's not about trying to stand *up*, it's about standing *in* — standing in Christ's strength. You may feel yourself being pushed around but you're still *in* His strength and *in* His mighty power. Don't trust *your* feelings of strength to stand, just stand in *His* strength by simply taking Him at His Word.

So do all you know to do to stand, then just stand! The evil attack you're going through won't last forever. Before you know it, the evil day will be over, and you'll be on your feet standing in another win!

PART III

Enjoying Our Victory in Christ in Everyday Life

Chapter 15

WALK IN THE VICTORY

Have you ever been going along enjoying the peace and victory you have in Christ, but then something came along that knocked you off your feet? Maybe it was a bad circumstance, an attack from the enemy, something someone did to you, or one of your own shortcomings or mistakes?

I remember being in a pool as a kid and getting on someone's shoulders and then attempting to stand up. I could stand up for a few seconds, but then I would fall in the water. That is the best way I can describe the struggle I dealt with for many years when it came to living in victory.

Every time I felt the effects of a new troubling situation — something the enemy did, something I did, or something someone did to me — I would pray and go back to God's Word and attempt to live in victory again.

But the victory would never last long. Just about the time I would start to enjoy victory, something would always knock me down again, restarting the process. I would pray, go back to God's Word, establish myself in what He said, and then "try" again. I would experience victory for just a short amount of time before I'd start to go down yet again.

No one can stand on another person's shoulders for very long. Similarly, this system I was operating in was never going to work because it wasn't intended to. It's a fun game in the pool, but no way to live your life.

The Lord began to teach me to stop trying to *get* the victory when situations knocked me down. He taught me to start using my faith to just *walk*.

Our victory, no matter what is going on in our lives (good or bad) is never based on our own worthiness. The scriptures point us to the fact that Jesus has already won the victory for us. And it is not something He needs to do again; He did it once for all time. Our challenge from here on out is to *walk* in that victory.

Although we may know and believe that Jesus won our victory, the fact of the matter is that we are sometimes tempted to give up. We're not tempted to give up on God or give up on our salvation, but we are tempted to give up the victory in a particular situation. We feel like a failure, so we feel like we need to get our victory again.

Those feelings of failure made me think I needed to pause my victory walk for a while. Gradually, I would establish myself in the victory again until the next thing in life knocked me off my feet. But to *walk* simply means to move along, to not stop. It really came as a surprise to me in that season of my life when the Lord began to encourage me over and over again to just *keep going*. Not to just keep going as in keep on living and breathing, but to keep going in the victory He provided for me.

So I want to say to you today that Jesus' victory is still true no matter what the circumstance is telling you. And He said to walk. Yes, the circumstances are bad, but walk!

If while attempting to walk in victory we make a mistake and commit sin, we will most likely deal with condemnation. Condemnation can really trip us up on our walk. I'd like to point out the difference between condemnation and conviction from the Holy Spirit.

Conviction comes when God shows us something we need to change. Condemnation comes when people judge us or when we are hard on ourselves because of something we need to change. Ultimately, condemnation comes from accusations against us from our spiritual enemy. (See John 16:8; Ephesians 4:30; 2 Corinthians 7:10; James 4:11–12; and Revelation 12:10.)

The Holy Spirit will gently convict us when we sin so we will repent and continue on our walk of victory. When we are experiencing condemnation we may repent, but we do not feel worthy to continue our victory walk. Although we may be tempted to hesitate in our walk, Hebrews 10:23 says, *"Let us hold on to the hope that we profess without the slightest hesitation ..."* (Phillips).

> *Stop trying to get the victory in your life and just walk!*

So when you sin, repent. Then — and here's the challenge — without the slightest hesitation, keep walking. Walk by spending time in prayer like you did before you missed the mark. Walk by claiming the promises just as strongly as you did before the attack came. Walk by enjoying Christ's victory even though you feel like a failure. Yes, you missed it and you'll miss it again, but walk! Walk! Keep moving.

Life is not a game of chicken in the pool, and neither is the victory your Savior provided for you. So stop trying to *get* the victory in your life and just *walk!*

CHAPTER 16

THRILL IN THE POWER

Growing up in church, I remember the powerful effect certain songs had on me. Every Easter, during the finale of my church's special presentation, a beautiful soprano voice would sing, "Jesus the resurrection, Jesus has given me life!" One of the most popular worship songs during my early teenage years was by the Imperials. They encouraged us to praise the Lord in our circumstances because "Jesus Christ has risen, so the work's already done!"[1] In the 1980s, singer and songwriter Carman recounted an imaginary conversation between Satan and the Grave after Jesus' death. The song built until the fear of Satan was realized when an angel announced Jesus was "alive and well with resurrection power!"[2] In more recent times, my heart has been uplifted as Kari Jobe sings, "The ground began to shake. The stone was rolled away. His perfect love could not be overcome. Now death where is your sting? Our resurrected King has rendered you defeated!"[3]

Why do songs like this lift our spirits in such an encouraging way? Because every one of those songs turns our thoughts toward not only the death and burial of Jesus but also the VICTORIOUS RESURRECTION of Jesus. No matter what we are going through, we can listen to a song about the resurrection of Jesus and thrill as we realize, "Yeah, that's right! Jesus has already won the victory!"

That resurrection power is not just something that happened 2,000 years ago. It is the truth of our Savior's current condition and position. He is *alive*, which means He is *living* in resurrection power. Think about that: He never leaves resurrection power; He lives in it.

But what does that have to do with what we're going through in our daily lives? Romans 5:10 (AMPC) says, *"For if while we were enemies we were reconciled to God through the death of His Son, it is much more [certain], now that we are reconciled, that we shall be saved (daily delivered from sin's dominion) through His [resurrection] life"* (emphasis added).

We have been saved through Jesus' death *and* saved by His resurrection life. The resurrection life He is living in right now is for our lives today.

Your victory is in the fact of the Lord's resurrection.

The resurrection of Christ is the highest realization any Christ follower can think about. There is nothing more thrilling, more glorious than this foundational, eternal truth. And once our spirits realize this fact, all else pales in comparison. It's kind of like homemade chocolate cake and icing. Once you've tasted it, no store-bought cake will be as good because you have tasted the best! I remember the first time I tasted homemade chocolate cake at a church potluck dinner. There was something different about that cake; it was the best I'd ever had. I was too young to know the difference between store-bought and homemade, but from then on it was always the "taste" I was looking for. Once your spirit gets a taste of this resurrection truth, nothing will be as glorious — your spirit will actually be craving more, to hear it again and again.

So don't wait until Easter to let your mind focus on Christ's resurrection. Take a verse, a message, or even a song that tells of His resurrection power and begin to think about this glorious truth. You may be in a situation that seems hopeless, just like the disciples' situation was during the days before Jesus rose from the dead. But the victory for your situation is the same as it was for theirs. Your victory is in the fact of the Lord's resurrection. Jesus is living to save you, so call on Him for whatever you need. He is living to help you today!

1. The Imperials. "Praise the Lord," from the album *Heed the Call*. Warner Chappell Music, Inc., 1979.
2. Carman. "Sundays on the Way (The Courtroom)," from the album *Sundays on the Way*. BMG Rights Management, 1983.
3. Kari Jobe. "Forever," from the album *Majestic*. Kari Jobe Carnes Music, 2014.

CHAPTER 17

LOOK UP AND INSIDE

In Luke 21, Jesus describes the evil that is coming on the earth and what to do when it happens. In verse 28 (MEV), He says, "When these things begin to happen, look up and lift up your heads, for your redemption is drawing near."

Where do you look when things go wrong in life? When things are going bad for us, we can quickly and directly go to our victory by looking at promises found in two places.

The first place we need to look, as this scripture says, is *up*. When we look up, we are looking at our high priest, Jesus, and His seating at the Father's right hand. Our help is going to come from the very throne of God! And when we look up, we see *where we really are*, our true spiritual position of being seated with Him. (See Hebrews 4:14–15 and Ephesians 1:20, 2:6.)

The second place we need to look is *inside*. We need to look inside of ourselves to see that the One Who lives in us is greater than the evil that is in this world (see 1 John 4:4).

We also look inside to see *who we really are*. He made us the righteousness of God in Christ. We really are His sons and daughters, and we are heirs of God. And because we are heirs, we can think about all He's provided for us in our salvation (see 2 Corinthians 5:21; Romans 8:17).

In life, it's natural for us to look *around*. But I want to give you some reasons we should look up and look inside — not look around us.

We see evil things happening all around us in the world, but if we dwell on these things, fear will begin to fill our hearts. Jesus said so in Luke 21:26 (KJV): *"Men's hearts failing them for fear, and for looking after those things which are coming on the earth ..."* As Christians, we do not need to fear what's happening in our world; we need to look up.

Looking up and looking inside keeps us from looking *around* at our circumstances and at any evil that may be trying to affect us. When we look around, we experience feelings of discouragement and defeat. But looking up and inside turns our attention away from the lies and toward the powerful truths of God's Word.

At times, it may seem helpful to look around to try to make ourselves feel better. We can "get out of the house," focus on work or education, hang out with friends, or entertain ourselves. Doing those things may help us feel better for a while, but they will not produce an assurance of victory about the situation. So we must intentionally look up and inside — not around at other things — to get us through. Choose to look up and inside *first*; that's living by faith.

> *Our victory is only found inside of us and above us.*

Another reason we need to look up and inside is because Satan is the god of this world (see 2 Corinthians 4:4). So if we look to this world for our help, our victory will never become a reality to us. This world has no victory for the believer. Our victory is only found inside of us and above us, where Jesus is ready to help and make His victory over the god of this world our reality.

But for us to *really* experience victory we need to *really* look up and inside at God's truths. Speaking of the Word of God, the apostle Peter tells us exactly how to do this: "... *You do well to pay [close] attention to it as to a lamp shining in a dark place, until the day dawns and light breaks through the gloom and the morning star arises in your hearts*" (2 Peter 1:19 AMP).

In other words, we keep looking at the truth until the light comes on in our hearts and breaks through the darkness of the hour. We know when the light comes on in our hearts; it's that moment when the Word of God becomes more real than our circumstances. That enlightenment is the result of *really* looking at the truth.

No matter how bad the world we live in gets, we can keep our minds in victory by looking up and looking inside!

CHAPTER 18

GO TO GOD'S WORDS

Jesus made an interesting statement the night He was betrayed and arrested. In His prayer to the Father, He said, *"But now I am coming to you, and I am saying these things in the world, so they may experience my joy completed in themselves"* (John 17:13 NET).

There was no joy in the moment He prayed that prayer. Jesus had told His disciples that He was sorrowful, even to the point of death. And while He prayed, the disciples slept because they were so sorrowful. Since we know the Bible says that both Jesus and the disciples were very sorrowful that night, we also know there was no joy in the moment He prayed that prayer. (See Mark 14:34 and Luke 22:45.)

So what did Jesus mean when He said, *"But now I am coming to you, and I am saying these things in the world,* so they may experience my joy completed in themselves"?

> Words make our joy complete, but not just any words — the Words of God.

Jesus meant that He was going to the Father but spoke words so that His followers would have His joy completed in them *after* He was gone. Words make our joy complete, but not just any words — the Words of God.

There have been times when I've been going through something and thought, "This time it's really bad. How am I going to make it?" But every one of those times, the help came through words, God's Words.

But the Word has no power to help us just sitting on the pages of our Bibles. There is a key we must use if we want these Words to produce joy in us. That key is found in Romans 15:13 (NKJV): *"Now may the God of hope fill you with all joy and peace in believing, that you may abound in hope by the power of the Holy Spirit."*

Believing is the key God uses to unlock the power of the Holy Spirit in our lives. The power of God brings us hope, joy, and peace when we believe the Word more than we believe our circumstances. Our believing releases the power of the Holy Spirit to bring this positive change in our emotions and outlook.

But it all starts with Words. Nothing spectacular or extraordinary, just simple Words. It always amazes me when I experience this powerful help from the Holy Spirit, knowing that it comes through the simple act of believing, even when at first it feels like this time the situation will require something more.

Jesus said His joy would be fulfilled in us through His Words. Although He spoke them more than 2,000 years ago, the Words of Christ are still for us today. Our wise Heavenly Father planned this means of daily victory knowing our life on earth would be a walk of faith fueled by Words.

So whether you're feeling down and need a little lift or just want to be filled with joy today, go to God's Words. Or maybe you feel like this time it's really bad, and surely you need something extraordinary to get you through. Go to God's Words, believe them, and then the empowerment will happen — hope, joy, and peace through the Holy Spirit.

CHAPTER 19

REMEMBER IT'S THE SAME

Have you ever seen one of those movies about a person having the same day over and over again? The alarm goes off, and the person wakes up and realizes that the day is the same as yesterday. As he continues on with his day, the same things that happened yesterday happen again, and he encounters the same situations with the same people as the day before. But it's not the next day; it's the same one again.

We see the person's confusion the first few times he lives the same day again, but eventually he begins to realize that he can actually use this experience for his own benefit and the benefit of others. The person knows what to say and what not to say, and he knows where and when to show up at just the right time. It's interesting to see how the movie plays out as the main character gets more and more perfected in his perpetual daily life.

In a similar way, Christ followers experience much of the same situations over and over again. Look at this passage from 1 Peter:

> **Be well balanced and always alert, because your enemy, the devil, roams around incessantly, like a roaring lion looking for its prey to devour. Take a decisive stand against him and resist his every attack with strong, vigorous faith. For you know that your believing brothers and sisters around the world are experiencing the same kinds of troubles you endure. And then, after your brief suffering, the God of all loving grace, who has called you to share in his eternal glory in Christ, will personally and powerfully restore you and make you stronger than ever ... (1 Peter 5:8–10 TPT)**

In verse 9, we see that our brothers and sisters in Christ are experiencing the same kinds of troubles we are. Believers were experiencing the same kinds of troubles when Peter wrote this passage 2,000 years ago, and believers are experiencing the same kinds of troubles today. These troubles will be the same throughout our lives.

Of course, we don't wake up every morning to the same day we had yesterday. But we do face the same troubles in our lives that we have been dealing with over and over again. The people and circumstances may be different, but the issues that troubles bring into our lives are the same: anxiety, fear, stress — the same, the same, the same.

What if we began to realize that the troubles we face are going to be the same for the rest of our lives? What if we woke up every morning — not hoping trouble won't happen again — but realizing that it's going to happen again? What if, when we encountered that same trouble, we chose to remember how the Lord helped us the last time we faced the same type of situation? I think that if we began to view trouble from this perspective, we would become skilled in our ability to resist our spiritual enemy.

We can take all those troubles we have already been through and apply the truth we stood on last time to this new situation. The circumstances may not be exactly the same, but the type of challenge is one we've walked through before. It's back again to bring us down; it's going to happen *again*. But here's the good news: Because the challenge is the same, we can apply the same winning strategy.

> *The truth of God's Word is the same as last time.*

If we won a victory by responding God's way the last time, then let's respond His way again. If we missed the mark in this area the last time, then we can strive to not make that mistake again. The truth of God's Word is the same as last time. It has the same wisdom as the last time we experienced the problem. When we apply the Word to the situation, the results will be the same every time — victory!

And as we respond God's way, the enemy will begin to realize *he* is going to experience the same treatment every time. The same resistance in Jesus' name, the same sword of the Spirit, the same defeat we dealt him before. The same, the same, the same!

CHAPTER 20

VIEW THE GLORY

An amazing passage in 2 Corinthians 3:7–11 says that when Moses came down from Mount Sinai with the Ten Commandments, the glory on his face was so bright that he had to cover his face with a veil. But as shining as Moses' face was, this passage says that the glory of the New Covenant is even *more* glorious. And just as the glory of the Old Covenant changed Moses, so the glory of the New Covenant changes us:

> **And all of us, as with unveiled face, [because we] continued to behold [in the Word of God] as in a mirror the glory of the Lord, are constantly being transfigured into His very own image in ever increasing splendor and from one degree of glory to another; [for this comes] from the Lord [Who is] the Spirit. (2 Corinthians 3:18 AMPC)**

This verse explains that as we continue to look at the glory of God in the Word of God, we are changed — even transfigured — into the image of Jesus. And the glory we are to constantly look at is the glory of this New Covenant found in the New Testament. The more we look at these truths, the more we are changed. And that changing makes us look more and more like Jesus.

But there's another huge bonus for the Christ follower who continues to look at New Testament truths. The very next verse in the Weymouth New Testament says, "Therefore, <u>while engaged in this service</u>, as we have experienced mercy <u>we do not lose heart</u>" (2 Corinthians 4:1 WNT 2012 ed., emphasis added). When we are engaged in looking at the truths of our salvation in the Word of God, we do not lose heart. The Good News Translation says it this way, "*God in his mercy has given us this work to do, and so we do not become discouraged.*"

The fact is we all get discouraged from time to time, but not *while* we are looking at the glories of the New Covenant. God has called every believer to look at the truths of our salvation. In this way, He has provided a safeguard against discouragement!

But when we are busy, preoccupied, or careless about spending time in these truths, we soon find ourselves getting discouraged. When this happens, we need to remember to focus on God's Word again.

Can looking at these truths actually change how we feel? Yes! Because we are looking at *glorious words*. They are truths of a New Covenant that God provided for us that is even more glorious than the glory of the Old

Covenant. So each truth comes with *glory*. No other words on earth come with such glory, *only* these New Covenant words.

> *No other words on earth come with such glory, only these New Covenant words.*

So keep looking at the glorious truth that God has delivered you from the power of darkness: *"He has delivered us from the power of darkness and has transferred us into the kingdom of His dear Son"* (Colossians 1:13 MEV).

Keep looking at the glorious truth that you are the righteousness of God in Christ: *"God made him who had no sin to be sin for us, so that in him we might become the righteousness of God"* (2 Corinthians 5:21 NIV).

Keep looking at the glorious truth that you are an heir of God and a co-heir with Christ: *"Now if we are children, then we are heirs — heirs of God and co-heirs with Christ, if indeed we share in his sufferings in order that we may also share in his glory"* (Romans 8:17 NIV).

Keep looking at the glorious truth that God is causing you to win in Christ: *"Now thanks be to God who always causes us to triumph in Christ and through us reveals the fragrance of His knowledge in every place"* (2 Corinthians 2:14 MEV).

Continually viewing the glory of the New Testament comes with a double blessing for us. We'll keep ourselves from discouragement as we journey through life while progressively changing to look more and more like Jesus!

CHAPTER 21

MAKE ROOM FOR VICTORY

Many of us have a favorite restaurant that has wonderful desserts. If our friends were eating dinner with us there for the first time, we might say to them, "Save room for dessert." We know that although the dinner may be delicious, our friends are really going to enjoy the special dessert, and we don't want them to miss out!

God does not want us to miss out on the victory Jesus paid such a high price to give us. The Bible says that when Jesus died and rose again, God completely defeated our spiritual enemy, forgave all our sins, raised us up with Jesus, and seated us with Jesus in heavenly places. (See Colossians 2:15, 1:14, 2:12 and Ephesians 2:4–6.)

I think we'd all like to experience more of this victory in our lives. But the first place that this victory is made real to us is in our own thoughts. The only way we can truly begin to experience what Jesus has given us is to renew our minds daily with victorious truths.

But the question is, how much time do we spend focusing on these amazing truths? Ephesians 4:23–24 (NET) says *"to be renewed in the spirit of your mind, and to put on the new man who has been created in God's image — in righteousness and holiness that comes from truth."*

> We put on the new man the same way we became a new man in Christ.

And how do we renew our minds? We renew our minds by filling our minds with God's Word through personal study or hearing Bible-based messages. But more specifically, we *put on* the new man the same way we *became* a new man in Christ. The Word tells us this:

> **If you say with your mouth that Jesus is Lord, and if you believe in your heart that God has raised Christ from death, you will be saved. A person believes with his heart, and he is made right with God. He speaks with his mouth and so is saved from his wrong ways. (Romans 10:9–10 WE)**

This is how we experienced our first spiritual victory — the victory of our salvation. Believing in our hearts and saying with our mouths brought us into our salvation, making it real and personal to us. And believing in our hearts and saying with our mouths will bring us into the *blessings* of our salvation, making each promise real and personal. So as we believe in our hearts and say with our mouths truths about our new lives, we are renewing our minds and putting on the new man. But we must *take time* to renew our minds to these truths.

The daily time we spend with our Heavenly Father can get filled up with Bible reading; worship; talking to Him about our day; sharing our needs, requests, and concerns; and thanking Him for all He has done. Before we know it, the time that we set aside is over and we need to go on with our busy day. If we do not renew our minds by considering our victory in Christ during this time with Him, we most likely won't do so any other time of the day. After all, this is usually the one part of our day that we devote to our spiritual life. So we must not forget to leave time for victory during our times with the Lord.

Our circumstances are always changing, and we will have needs and problems to pray about every day of our lives. *But our victory never changes.* It remains as glorious as the day Jesus rose from the dead. When we give our minds a taste of this truth, we always want more! Just like a person with a sweet tooth needs a little more to complete a good meal, we need to have a taste for victory in our time with God that is not satisfied unless we give time to victorious truths!

We give our minds this taste of victory every time we renew it with truths such as 1 Corinthians 15:57 (MEV), which says, *"But thanks be to God, who gives us the victory through our Lord Jesus Christ!"* As our minds begin to chew on this truth, a new attitude is formed — one that realizes that no matter what our day holds, victory *will* be given to us through Christ!

We can experience more of Jesus' victory in our lives by renewing our minds to the truths of victory in the Word of God. Then we can go about our day enjoying a victorious attitude. So in your time with God, save room for victory!

CONCLUSION

In Luke, we see a story of how Jesus faced a potentially fearful situation:

> **At that time some Pharisees came to Jesus and said to him, "Leave this place and go somewhere else. Herod wants to kill you." He replied, "Go tell that fox, 'I will keep on driving out demons and healing people today and tomorrow, and on the third day I will reach my goal.' In any case, I must press on today and tomorrow and the next day — for surely no prophet can die outside Jerusalem!" (Luke 13:31–33 NIV)**

Jesus was giving us an example of how to handle attacks from our spiritual enemy. When Satan attacks our minds with fear, we can proclaim, like Jesus did, that we will continue to do what God has called us to do in life. Just as Jesus pointed to the supernatural works He was doing, we can point to our purpose in life when the enemy comes and tells us we're not going to make it. If you're unclear about what your purpose is, go to the Word of God and, in faith, proclaim promises such as this one: *"God began doing a good work in you, and I am* sure he will continue it until it is finished when Jesus Christ comes again" (Philippians 1:6 NCV).

But Jesus did more than point to the great supernatural events happening in the course of His life. He pointed to what He was doing daily to ensure God's purpose would be fulfilled. He said, *"I must press on today and tomorrow and the next day."* He knew that His life was not just a series of supernatural events. It was also a daily walk, one that He had to continue until it was time for Him to go to the cross.

Now it's our turn. We must keep going and press on today, tomorrow, and the next day — until we have finished our race.

I mentioned in the introduction the importance of using our faith on our spiritual journey. We use our faith by believing God's Word more than we believe our circumstances, feelings, and mental reasoning. As I pointed out, the *only* way we can achieve victory over the evil in this world is through our faith: *"For every child of God defeats this evil world, and we achieve this victory through <u>our faith</u>"* (1 John 5:4 NLT, emphasis added).

Hebrews 12:2 says, *"Looking to Jesus, the <u>author and finisher of our faith</u>, who for the joy that was set before him suffered the cross, disregarding the shame, and is seated on the right hand of the throne of God"* (NMB, emphasis added).

Jesus is the author of our faith. He was there at the beginning of our spiritual journey, and He continues with us as we learn to understand our victory, use our victory, and enjoy our victory in everyday life. But He is also the finisher of our faith. In Revelation 22:13 (MEV), Jesus tells us, "*I am the Alpha and the Omega, the Beginning and the End, the First and the Last.*"

Many times in an athletic race, runners receive encouragement from friends and family at the start line who cheer them on as they begin their race. But while the athletes continue to run, those cheering for them move to the finish line to cheer them on during the very end of their race. In a similar way, Jesus was with us at the beginning of our spiritual journey, cheering us on.

But He didn't stay at the starting line of our journey, because He is "the Beginning and *the End*." He has planned a great victory for us when we cross over that finish line. And He's there, standing at the end of our race and cheering us on. He sees what's ahead of us — the obstacles and the twists and turns of our road — and yet yells out, "You can do it! Don't give up! I'm calling from the finish line, and I say that YOU WIN!"

ABOUT THE AUTHOR

Stephanie Trayers and her husband, Eddie Trayers, are the lead pastors of Summit Church, a thriving multicultural congregation in the Washington, D.C., metropolitan area. Stephanie is an avid teacher, sharing with the Summit community the basics that bring everyday sustaining power for the follower of Jesus Christ. She demonstrates a lifestyle of connection to God through her example of a life of prayer, and she makes a purposeful impact in the lives of the people of Summit Church. She enjoys reading, baking, and spending time in the mountains of Virginia. Eddie and Stephanie have been married for more than 30 years, and they have two grown daughters, Tori and Megan.

Made in the USA
Middletown, DE
21 June 2024